Ribbon Trims

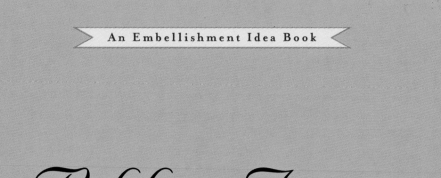

An Embellishment Idea Book

Ribbon Trims

NANCY NEHRING

The Taunton Press

Publisher
Jim Childs

Acquisitions Editor
Jolynn Gower

Editorial Assistant
Sarah Coe

Copy Editor
Candace B. Levy

Designer/Layout Artist
Lisa Sloane

Photographer
Jack Deutsch

Illustrator
Ronald Carboni

The Taunton Press

Printed in Singapore
10 9 8 7 6 5 4 3 2 1

The Taunton Press, Inc.
63 South Main Street, PO Box 5506
Newtown, CT 06470-5506
e-mail: tp@taunton.com
Distributed by Publishers Group West

Library of Congress Cataloging-in-Publication Data
Nehring, Nancy.
Ribbon trims / Nancy Nehring.
p.   cm.
"An embellishment idea book."
ISBN 1-56158-308-1
1. Dressmaking. 2. Clothing and dress—Decoration. 3. Ribbons.
4. Fancy work. I. Title.
TT552.N44 1999
646.4—dc21   99-18060
                                                      CIP

The Victorian era, the heyday of textile arts, is now 100 to 150 years in the past. Textiles, although durable goods, are certainly not permanent. Written instructions for Victorian textile arts were rare and often consisted of a tiny engraving of the finished piece.

I'd like to dedicate this book to those today who are helping to preserve Victorian textile arts through research, reproduction, written instruction, and use before these arts are lost.

Contents

INTRODUCTION   viii

1. THE BASICS   3

Ribbon Types   4

Make Your Own Ribbon   6

Getting Started   7

Measuring Ribbon   10

Ending   12

Cleaning and Storing
Ribbon Trims   14

2. QUILLED RIBBON TRIMS   17

Edge-Stitched Knife Pleats   18

Knife Pleats with Both
Edges Stitched   22

Edge-Stitched Double and
Triple Knife Pleats   24

Center-Stitched Knife
Pleats   26

Center-Stitched Double and
Triple Knife Pleats   28

Bent Knife Pleats   30

Pleated Scallops   32

Center-Stitched Box Pleats   35

Edge-Stitched Box Pleats   38

Box Pleats with Both
Edges Stitched   40

Edge-Stitched Double and
Triple Box Pleats   42

Center-Stitched Double and
Triple Box Pleats   44

Paddlewheels   47

Pulled Box Plaits   50

Maltese Cross Plaits   52

Bow Ties   54

Tiny Bows   56

Flying Geese   58

Diamonds and Squares	60	Flutes	100
Hexagons	62	Ribbons and Bows	102
Fans	64		
Rosettes	66	**4. SMOGKED AND LOOPED**	
Arrows	68	**RIBBON TRIMS**	107
		Shell Smocking	108
3. RUCHED RIBBON TRIMS	71	Lattice Smocking	110
Edge Gather	72	Looped Ribbon	112
Center Gather	74	Two-Ribbon Looped Trim	114
Three-Layer Ruffle	76		
Multiple Gathers	78	**5. TWISTED RIBBON TRIMS**	117
Gathers and Spaces	80	Making Twisted	
Shirred Gather	82	Ribbon Trims	118
Shells	84	Zigzag Twist	120
Half-Shells	86	Ribbon Prairie Points	122
Scalloped Edge	88	Diamond Fence Rail	124
Semicircles	90	Square Fence Rail	126
Tucked Gather	92	Alternating Stripes	128
Corded Gather	94	Shark's Teeth	130
Beading	96		
Circles and Dots	98	**SOURCES**	133

Introduction

RICK RACK ISN'T THE RIGHT TRIM FOR THAT EVENING DRESS you're making? Satin ribbon with lace edges won't do on that wool tweed suit? Can't ever find the right color or texture of ribbon that you want? Well, you can make your own ribbon trims and even your own ribbon and not be limited to the generic trims and standard materials that you find in the fabric store.

Ribbon trims are long lengths of ribbon that are gathered, pleated, twisted, or looped into decorative trims. Ribbon trims can be made in

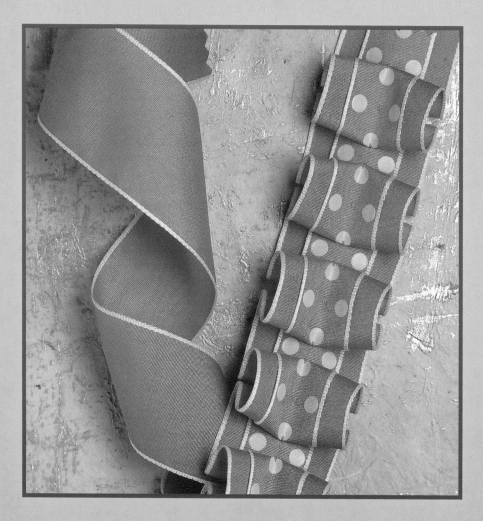

any size, shape, and color you might want. They have real personalities—frilly, feminine, sexy, sophisticated—so one is always right for whatever use you have in mind.

Occasionally, a ribbon trim is the focal point of a design, but more often it is the glue that ties different elements of the design together. Trims accent other design features. When used between motifs or sections, trims lead the eye from one to the next. A trim finishes an edge, such as a sleeve or hem, and leads the eye around, holding attention on the design. Trims can frame a face, either from the neck edge or from the edge on a hat.

This book is a collection of my favorite trims with step-by-step instructions that tell you how to make each one. Many of the trims are shown in a fancy ribbon, accented with beads, buttons, or other small objects, or combined with lace, braid, or other ribbons to help you imagine the variety of ways each trim might be used.

My inspiration comes from eighteenth-, nineteenth-, and early-twentieth-century clothing, which was often decorated with ribbon trims, and from my collection of Victorian fashion books. The patterns were collected one at a time and often consisted of a close-up photo of a museum piece or an engraving in an old book. I felt I had hit pay dirt the day I found five trims on a single page in an 1867 Godey's Ladies Book. Even then, in typical Victorian fashion, the complete instructions consisted of a one-page engraving of the finished pieces.

The samples shown in this book are made from ribbons purchased in chain fabric and craft stores. Like fabric, ribbons have a fashion season. The colors, textures, and designs change frequently. So don't expect to reproduce the examples here exactly. Use them as guides for making your own unique trims. Also, specialty shops, flea markets, mail-order sources, and the Internet are good places to look for more varieties of ribbon.

Enjoy!

The Basics

RIBBON TRIMS ARE EASY TO MAKE and have lots of wonderful uses. With a few simple hints on selecting ribbon, getting started, and ending, you will be creating your own ribbon trims in just a few minutes. Whether you need just a few inches or many yards, ribbon trims make up quickly and give a finishing touch to numerous clothing, accessory, furnishing, and gift items.

Ribbons have long been used to beautify our clothing and accessories. Since their invention in the fifteenth century, ribbons had always been confined to use by the upper classes, either by cost or by sumptuary laws. The morning dresses, tea dresses, walking dresses, and evening dresses of the Victorian upper class, which were lavishly trimmed, became outdated as lifestyles changed and as the middle class grew more numerous and prospered. As women's dress became more simplified and streamlined after World War I, the use of ribbons began to decline. Today, ribbons are no longer a sign of wealth but are a sign of femininity and sexuality, as they are used mostly on girl's clothing, women's lingerie, underwear, special-occasion dresses, and accessories. Here are some ideas for using ribbon trims.

feminine garments—insertions for heirloom sewing, lingerie, formals, ruffles on tuxedo shirts

wedding and bridal shower—veils, hats, flower girl's basket, ring bearer's pillow, garters, table decorations (for example, bunting and fake cake trimmed with ribbons that look like frosting decorations)

baby clothes and accessories—bassinet trim, christening gown and cap, baby bonnet, headbands for little girls with no hair

hair accessories—barrettes, headbands, snoods

hats—hat bands, edge trims

purses—body of bag, insertion in body of bag, appliquéd trim

jewelry—chokers, belts, shoe trims

dolls—clothing, accessories, dollhouse furnishings

costumes—historical; fantasy; Halloween costumes, masks, wands

household furnishings—pillows, footstools, drapes, curtains, tie backs, slipcovers, lamp shades

household accessories—fabric-covered boxes, picture frames, baskets

holiday and party decorations—bunting, Christmas garlands and ornaments, package decorations, streamers

awards and sashes—ribbons for competitions, sashes for dignitaries

RIBBON TYPES

There are many types of ribbon on the market today, and ribbon trims can be made from many of these. Traditional woven ribbons of satin, taffeta, organdy, grosgrain, and velvet are suitable for any of the trims shown in this book. Woven ribbons are made from both natural and synthetic fibers, including silk, rayon, cotton, polyester, acetate, nylon, and Lurex.

Cut ribbon, or craft ribbon, is fabric that has been cut into ribbon widths (instead of woven to the desired width) and stiffened to

prevent raveling. It can't be manipulated into gathers or smocked but can be used for some of the quilled and twisted ribbon trims.

Wire-edged ribbons, usually of silk or acetate taffeta, can be used for some gathered trims with one or both of the wires in place; but for many of the trims shown here, you'll need to remove the wires. Remove the wire as follows: Push the tip of the wire out from the selvage of the ribbon and grab the end with tweezers. Gather the ribbon along the wire to expose more wire. Secure the wire end around a solid, heavy object, such as shears, a door knob, or a metal chair leg. Continue gathering the ribbon along the wire, eventually pushing ribbon off the opposite end of the wire. For very long pieces of ribbon, you can push the wire out of the selvage every few feet, cut the wire, and work the ribbon off the wire in smaller lengths.

Any width of ribbon $\frac{1}{4}$ in. or larger can be used to create ribbon trims. Today ribbons typically come in widths up to 3 in. wide. Wider ribbons are sometimes available from specialty stores, or you can make your own. The width you choose for a particular trim is determined by the scale of the article being trimmed. For this reason, the ribbon width (RW) is the basic unit of measure when creating ribbon trims.

MAKE YOUR OWN RIBBON

If you can't find the ribbon you want, whether it's the color, fiber, or width that's wrong, you can create your own. Choose a fabric based on the weight, stiffness, texture, color, and fiber content for the ribbon you desire. The following fabrics make beautiful ribbons for trims: bengaline (same as grosgrain but in wider widths), shantung, bridal satin, moiré satin, organdy, decorator moiré, taffeta, cotton lawn, velvet, eyelet, seersucker, dotted Swiss, sheer polyester, and net. Many other fabrics also work well.

A fabric's stiffness can sometimes be altered. A flimsy fabric can be stiffened by using two layers of fabric or fabric and iron-on interfacing. Fuse two layers of fabric together with fusible web, or fuse the fabric to the iron-on interfacing. A stiff fabric can sometimes be made softer by washing.

To make ribbon, mark the fabric to the desired width; then cut the fabric and finish the edges. There are a variety of ways to finish the edges. Choose one depending on the use of the finished trim.

The fastest edge finish is made by cutting the fabric with pinking shears. Historically, this was a common method used in the eighteenth and nineteenth centuries to create ribbon from leftover fabric for dress trims. A pinker, which looks like a small branding iron, was struck with a hammer to cut the fabric. This is not a very durable edge and is not appropriate for ribbon trims that will receive hard use.

For a fast, plain edge, the fabric can be cut with a rotary cutter or shears and sealed with a fabric sealant. Test the sealant on a scrap first, because it may discolor the fabric.

The most durable edges are hemmed edges. The fastest of these is a narrow serged edge. Many sergers have a narrow two-thread hem, which is perfect for creating ribbons. Mark the ribbon width on the fabric, and the serger will cut and hem in one operation. Metallic or novelty thread can be used for a contrasting edge.

Finally, a narrow rolled hem can finish the edges. A straight stitch, decorative stitch, or blindstitch done by either machine or hand can be used to create a variety of narrow hems.

GETTING STARTED

It's easy to get started making ribbon trims. You need only four things—ribbon, needle, thread, and small scissors. An estimate of how much ribbon you need for a finished length of trim is given in the instructions for each trim. You may need more or less, depending on how close together you space the motifs or, in some instances, the width of the ribbon you chose. The trims don't take much room to make so they are great take-along work for the car, airplane, doctor's office, or kids' soccer practice.

I usually hand-stitch my trims, but trims using running stitches can often be machine-stitched. When hand-stitching, I use regular sewing or quilting thread. Whether I use a single or double strand depends on the weight of the ribbon and the weight of the thread. For lightweight sheers and silks, I use a double strand of sewing thread or

a single strand of quilting thread. For heavier ribbons, such as grosgrain and velvet, I use a double strand of quilting thread.

Discrete stitches hold the trims together, and stitching is simple. It consists of either long lines of running stitch or small individual tacks. Begin the running stitch with a backstitch. A thread with a single knot in the end will pull right through most ribbons. To make the backstitch, bring the needle and thread up through the fabric, go down one stitch width away, and then come back up in the same spot as before. Then you are ready to begin the running stitch by going in and out of the fabric. The running stitch does not need to be very consistent in length but it does need to stay on the stitching line. Because the ribbons are so narrow, a small deviation from the stitching line can consume a significant portion of the ribbon width, causing the trim to be lopsided.

Tacks are equally simple to make. Bring the needle and thread up through the fabric, usually at the fold of a pleat. Go back down about ⅛ in. away, usually just off the edge of the pleat. Repeat coming up and going down in the same holes used the first time. Tie off on the back, and cut the thread.

Stitches and tacks show on many of the trims. Use thread in a matching color, and make neat stitches. As long as the stitches are neat and even, they will not detract from the finished trim.

Machine-stitching narrow ribbons can be tricky. Fabrics used to make ribbons—such as satins, velvets, and organdies—are difficult to sew, even when not layered high or gathered. To avoid problems, try these suggestions. Start with a new, sharp needle. Even a slightly dull needle or a needle with a burr will snag tightly woven ribbons, such as satin and grosgrain. Use quilting thread for both needle and bobbin threads when sewing through multiple layers or when gathering heavy ribbon, such as grosgrain. Place tear-away interfacing under the ribbon to keep the ribbon from sinking beneath the throat plate (especially at the beginning of a stitching line) and to keep the ribbon from slipping as it feeds under the presser foot. You can even mark foldlines for the ribbon on the interfacing. Use a large straight pin or laying tool to hold the ribbon in position as it feeds under the presser foot. Don't sew over pins, as the pins can permanently dent the fabric. When stitching gathering lines, loosen the top tension slightly and then pull up on the bobbin thread only. You can gather a long length in just seconds.

Ribbon trims can be embellished with beads, nail heads, sequins, metallic threads, and ribbon motifs (such as ribbon roses). Often the embellishment can be sewn on the trim at the same time you are completing another step. For instance, beads and ribbon roses can be sewn on when tacks are made. Other embellishments can be sewn on using the same stitches used to sew the trim to a garment.

The trims combine well with lace and braids. Ribbon and lace can be stacked and treated as one unit to form trims. In fact, lace alone or even bias tubes of fabric can be substituted for ribbon to create trims. Braids are too stiff to form trims, but they can often be edged with ribbon trims or used to embellish a trim.

Most of the ribbon trims are easy to apply. The trims can be sewn or glued into place. Try to sew or glue along a stitching line, behind a pleat, at a tack, or on the back layer of a trim with multiple layers. Because the trims are gathered along a single thread or held together with occasional tacks, most trims are very flexible and will bend around curves easily. If you need to go around a sharp corner, you can adjust the length of three or four repeats of the trim motif so the pattern breaks exactly at the corner.

MEASURING RIBBON

For a neat appearance, the repeating motifs that make up the ribbon trim need to be of consistent size. Measurements in the instructions for motif size, stitching line lengths, foldlines, and distances between motifs are not given in absolute lengths but are given in fractions or multiples of the ribbon width (RW). This is because most trims can be made from any size of ribbon; and an absolute measurement such as 1 in. is, in practical terms, a long distance on a $\frac{1}{4}$-in.-wide ribbon but only a short distance on a 3-in.-wide ribbon. The ribbon width is the distance from one selvage of the ribbon to the other.

There are three ways to measure RW while forming motifs. As you might expect, each method has its advantages and disadvantages, but often more than one method can be used to form a single trim. Sometimes one method will be recommended for a certain trim because it is easier to obtain good results using that method.

You will be able to judge the RW or multiple that you are using quite accurately after you have completed a few motifs. For trims that do not require strict accuracy, you can eventually work "by feel," without having to measure every increment.

Measure with a ruler

The most obvious method of measuring ribbon is to use a ruler. Mark the necessary RWs on the ribbon with a pencil, air-disappearing marker, or straight pins.

Measure by folding the ribbon

You can use the ribbon itself as a measuring device. At one end of the ribbon, fold the ribbon, following the diagram, to determine RW or a multiple of it. If you'd like, you can mark or press the required measurements into the ribbon. Hold the marked ribbon end up to the other end of the ribbon to measure and form the trim.

For 1 RW, fold the ribbon on a diagonal (45 degrees) and mark where the ribbon edge touches the opposite edge. Folds for measuring ½, 1, 2, and 3 RWs are shown.

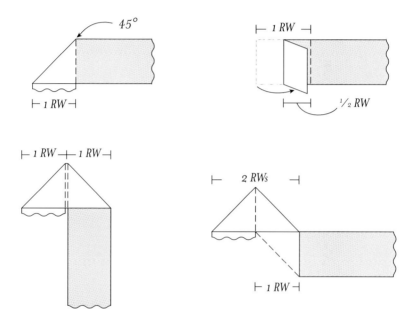

Measure with gauges

The gauge method is used for pleated and twisted trims that are composed of folded ribbon. The gauges themselves are strips of lightweight card stock, thin plastic, or other material cut to the exact shape of each motif component. Gauges are an accurate way to measure ribbon but are time-consuming to prepare and require manipulating several components at one time, because often several gauges are stacked with ribbon folded between them. The motif or partial motif is secured with stitching. Then the gauges are removed and reused for the next motif.

Prepare the gauges by first forming one motif to your liking using the ruler or folded ribbon method of measurement. Press this motif flat with a steam iron so all of the folds are sharply creased. Unfold the ribbon and very accurately trace the shape of each section of ribbon between any two folds onto your gauge material (for example, card stock). You may also need gauges that cover the area from the first and last folds to the edge of the motif. Finally, make a duplicate of the first gauge (and possibly the whole set) so you can space and start the second motif before removing all of the gauges from the first.

To use the gauges, lay each gauge on the ribbon in order, folding the ribbon as required between each gauge. Stitch the folds in place. If you find you can't stitch the motif with the gauges in place, press the folds with the gauges in place, remove the gauges, refold the motif, and stitch the folds. The trim "Edge-Stitched Knife Pleats" (p. 18) demonstrates the use of gauges.

ENDING

Most ribbon ends fray when cut, so the ends need to be covered or finished to keep the ribbon trim looking neat. One of the following techniques will give a finished look to your trim.

For continuous trims, the ends can be hidden. Turn the ends behind the trim and secure. If the trim crosses a seam on a garment, the ends can be sewn into the seam. To match the motifs and make the trim look continuous, adjust the size of the last three or four motifs to fill the space exactly.

Trims that end at seams in a garment can be finished by sewing the ribbon ends into the seam. If the ribbon is too bulky to be stitched in the seams, fold the end under the trim and stitch down.

For nonclothing items or garments for which the end is in the middle of the fabric, fold the raw edge under or finish by using one of the decorative ends presented on the facing page and p. 14.

Square folded end

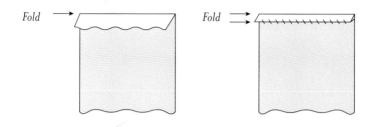

A square folded end is created by first cutting the ribbon perpendicular to the selvages. Then fold the end over twice and blindstitch.

Pointed folded end

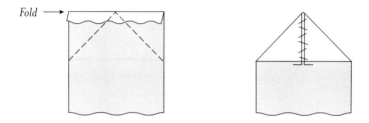

A pointed folded end is created by first cutting the ribbon perpendicular to the selvages. Fold the end over once. Then fold the corners in until they meet at the center back. Stitch at the center back where the two halves of the first fold meet.

Diagonal folded end

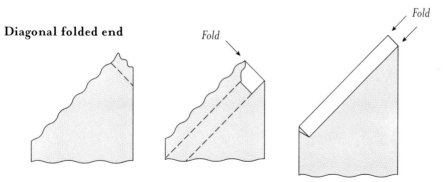

A diagonal folded end begins by trimming the ribbon end at 45 degrees. Next trim the tip of the ribbon off perpendicular to the 45-degree cut. Fold the tip in; then fold the diagonal cut over twice. Blindstitch the diagonal fold.

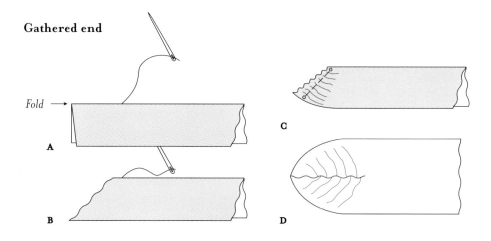

Gathered end

Fold →

A

B

C

D

A gathered end provides a softer end than do the folded ends. Fold the end of the ribbon in half and stitch at 45 degrees, starting at the selvages and angling away from the cut end. Hold the needle and thread out of the way and trim off the excess ribbon. Pull up on the thread to gather, and tie off. Adjust the gathers evenly, and unfold the end.

CLEANING AND STORING RIBBON TRIMS

Many items that use ribbon trims can be cleaned just by brushing to remove any dust. But some items, garments in particular, need to be cleaned more thoroughly. A few ribbon trims, such as those made with stiffer grosgrain ribbon, can be hand-washed and drip dried. While the trim is drying, reshape it with your fingers. Be sure you prewash the ribbon before making the trim. Some ribbons, such as those made from satin, wrinkle badly when washed and can't be ironed after the trim is formed. Others can be dry cleaned, but the garment must be ironed by hand so the trim isn't crushed. If in doubt, make a small sample of the ribbon trim and clean it to see how it holds up. Trims that don't clean well can be mounted on hook-and-loop tape or snap tape and removed before the garment is cleaned.

When storing items with ribbon trims, pad the trim so it won't be crushed. Crumpled tissue paper on either side of the trim will safeguard it. Plastic foam packing peanuts will work for boxed items, if the peanuts themselves are not crushed down tightly.

2

Quilled Ribbon Trims

QUILLED RIBBON TRIMS have a formal, tailored look. They are formed from soft (unpressed) pleats, which are stacked, tacked, and lifted into complex three-dimensional shapes. The technique gobbles up yardage, using three to seven times the length of the finished trim.

Any type of ribbon can be used to make quilled ribbon trims. Grosgrain is my favorite because the grain is prominent, making it easy to form straight pleats. These trims are especially effective if there is a different color on the reverse side of the ribbon; an alternative is to hold two different colored ribbons together and treat them as one while creating the motifs. The pleats are held with tacks or running stitches.

Edge-Stitched
Knife Pleats

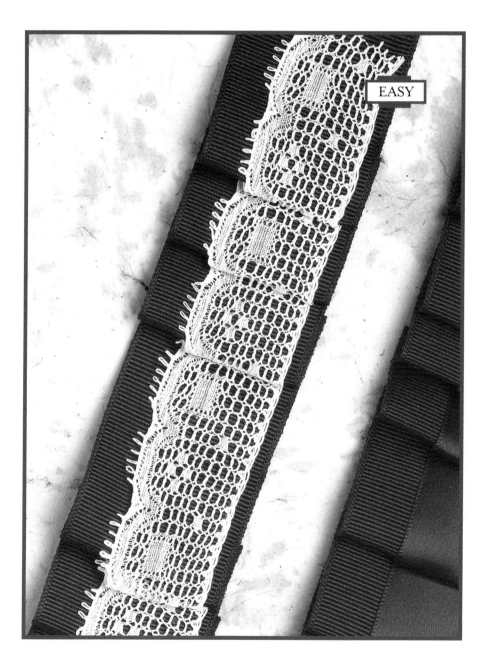

EASY

INSTRUCTIONS

Use a ribbon that's 3X the length of the finished trim. This trim can be machine-stitched. Any of the methods for measuring ribbon can be used to make knife pleats (see "Measuring Ribbon" on p. 10). The example shown here demonstrates the gauge method.

1 Cut four gauges from lightweight card stock or plastic. The gauges should be the width of the desired pleat and should be as long as the ribbon is wide.

2 With ribbon right side up, place the first gauge on the ribbon so it covers about three-quarters the width of the ribbon. Fold the ribbon over the gauge.

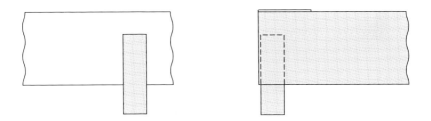

3 Place a second gauge on top of the first. There will be one layer of ribbon between the gauges. Fold the ribbon back over the second gauge. This forms the first pleat.

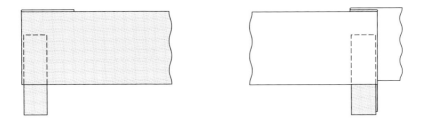

4 Lay the third gauge on top of the ribbon, butting it up next to the first two gauges. Fold the ribbon over the gauge.

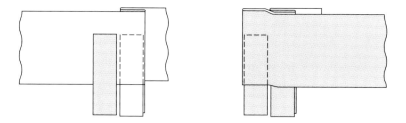

5 Place the last gauge on top of the third gauge and the ribbon. Fold the ribbon over the fourth gauge. This forms the second pleat.

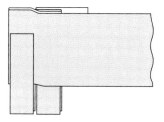

6 Stitch the pleats in place along the selvage.

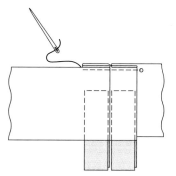

7 Remove the gauges from the first pleat and use them to form the next pleat.

8 Stitch the newly formed pleat in place along one selvage.

9 Continue moving the gauges and stitching the pleats in place until the desired length is achieved.

VARIATIONS

- ◆ Vary the width and spacing of the pleats.
- ◆ Group three to five knife pleats, then leave a space.
- ◆ Alternate wide and narrow pleats, using two sizes of gauges.
- ◆ Layer two different width ribbons or ribbon and lace and treat them as one while forming pleats.

Press the pleats if you want crisp folds.

Knife Pleats with
Both Edges Stitched

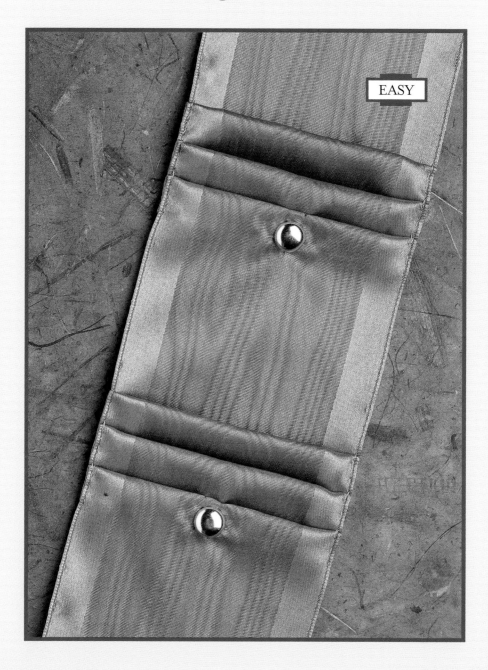

EASY

INSTRUCTIONS

Use a ribbon that's 3X the length of the finished trim. This trim can be machine-stitched. You can make this knife pleat with a narrow silk ribbon and use it as an insertion for French hand sewing.

Knife pleats with both edges stitched are usually used for insertions in which both edges are covered, so a continuous stitch is used. Tacks can be used if they're more appropriate for your application.

Form pleats as directed in "Edge-Stitched Knife Pleats" (p. 18). After removing the gauges in Step 7, stitch the pleat down on the second edge. Follow the grain of the ribbon to keep the pleat even from selvage to selvage.

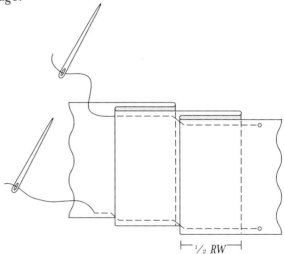

$\vdash$ ½ RW $\dashv$

VARIATIONS

- ◆ Vary the width and spacing of the pleats.
- ◆ Group three to five pleats, then leave a space.
- ◆ Alternate wide and narrow pleats.

Don't press this trim. Pressed pleats flatten out and look like seams instead of pleats.

Edge-Stitched Double and Triple Knife Pleats

EASY

INSTRUCTIONS

For double pleats, use a ribbon that's 5X the length of the finished trim. For triple pleats, use a ribbon that's 7X the finished length. This trim can be machine-stitched.

Double and triple knife pleats look best when made with ribbon that is at least 2 in. wide. This allows the edges to fan out.

Any method of measuring can be used (see "Measuring Ribbon" on p. 10). For the gauge method, six gauges are needed for double pleats and eight for triple pleats.

Form the pleats as directed in "Edge-Stitched Knife Pleats" (p. 18), except stack two or three pleats in place on top of each other and edgestitch before moving to the next pleat.

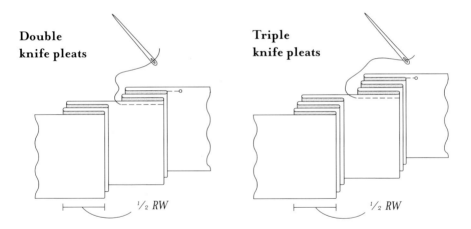

Double knife pleats

Triple knife pleats

½ RW

½ RW

Tacks can be used if more appropriate for your application, but the stitched edge is usually covered and the continuous stitch is more secure. Stitch tacks at both left and right edges.

VARIATIONS

- Graduate the size of the pleats within the stack.
- Vary the distance between adjacent pleats.

This trim can be used in place of fringe for a more sophisticated look in home decorating.

Center-Stitched
Knife Pleats

EASY

INSTRUCTIONS

Use a ribbon that's 3X the length of the finished trim. This trim can be machine-stitched.

1 Fold the ribbon right sides together.

2 From the fold, measure ½ RW. Fold the ribbon wrong sides together.

3 Stitch in the center on either side of the pleat with tacks or stitch with continuous stitching down the centerline.

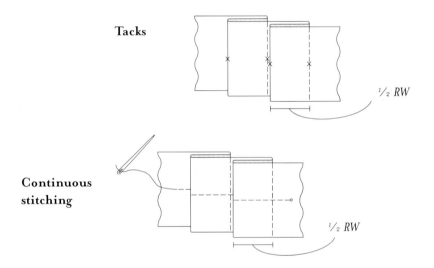

Tacks

½ RW

Continuous stitching

½ RW

4 Repeat until desired length is achieved. To make pleats that touch, place the first fold of the next pleat 1 RW from the last fold.

When stitching by machine, stitch with the top of the fold toward you, so the fold won't catch on the presser foot.

VARIATIONS

 ◆ Vary the width of the pleats.
 ◆ Alternate narrow and wide pleats.
 ◆ Vary the spacing of the pleats; they can be spaced farther apart or can even overlap.

Center-Stitched Double and Triple Knife Pleats

EASY

INSTRUCTIONS

For double pleats, use a ribbon that's 5X the length of the finished trim. For triple pleats, use a length of ribbon that's 7X the finished length. This trim can be machine-stitched.

Form pleats as directed in "Center-Stitched Knife Pleats" (p. 26), except stack two or three pleats and stitch in place before proceeding to the next pleat. The pleats can be stitched with either tacks or continuous stitching.

Tacks

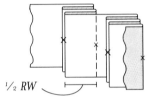

double knife pleats

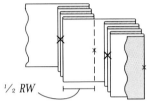

triple knife pleats

Continuous stitching

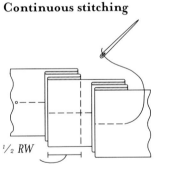

double knife pleats

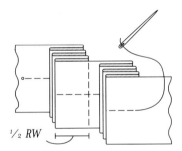

triple knife pleats

VARIATIONS

- ◆ Space the pleats farther apart.
- ◆ Alternate single pleats with double or triple pleats.
- ◆ Graduate the width of the pleats; the smaller pleats should be on top of the stack.

These trims are very full. You may need to press the pleats to tame them. The wider the ribbon, the flatter the pleats lie.

Bent Knife Pleats

EASY

INSTRUCTIONS

Use a ribbon that's 3X the length of the finished trim.

1 Form a knife pleat ⅓ RW wide. To make this trim using gauges, follow Steps 1 to 3 for "Edge-Stitched Knife Pleats" (p. 18).

2 Pull the top edge of the fold about ¼ RW toward the center of the ribbon, and tack it along the selvage. Remove the gauges, if using.

3 Repeat Step 2 on the bottom edge of the fold. The center of the pleat will bend upward, forming a peak.

4 Begin the next pleat immediately adjacent to the one just formed.

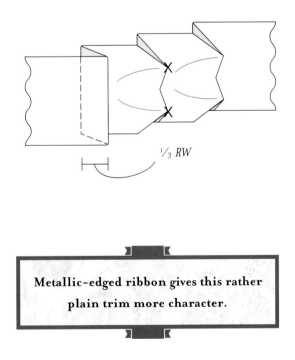

⅓ RW

Metallic-edged ribbon gives this rather
plain trim more character.

Pleated Scallops

INTERMEDIATE

INSTRUCTIONS

Use a ribbon that's 4X the length of the finished trim. This trim can be machine-stitched.

For the pleated scallop trim shown in the photo, I used Offray Aria ribbon, ³⁄₈-in. and ³⁄₁₆-in. gauges (see "Measuring Ribbon" on p. 10), braid, and gold seed beads. Aria ribbon allows you to finger-press the folds, whereas most other ribbons require you to steam-press the folds.

Press ³⁄₁₆-in. knife pleats into the ribbon as follows.

1   Make a fold in the ribbon with right sides together.

2   Place a ³⁄₈-in. gauge along the fold, and fold the ribbon over the gauge with wrong sides together.

3   Place a ³⁄₁₆-in. gauge along the fold, and fold the ribbon over the gauge with right sides together. Press.

4   Place a ³⁄₈-in. gauge along fold you just made. Fold the ribbon over the gauge.

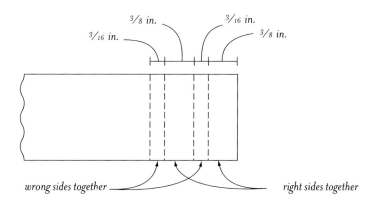

5 Continue in this pattern, repeating the steps and keeping the selvages even, until the desired length has been made.

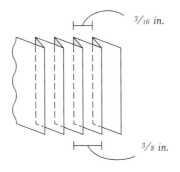

6 Spread the pleated ribbon widthwise so that every sixth pleat is a point or valley of a scallop. Backstitch down the centerline to hold each pleat in place.

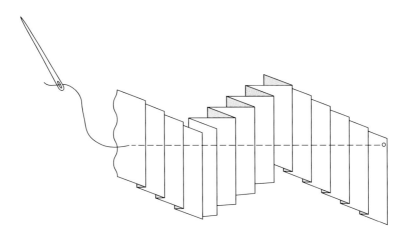

7 Blindstitch the braid on top of the centerline to cover the stitching. Highlight the braid with seed beads.

VARIATIONS

- ◆ Make the pleats wider.
- ◆ Use more pleats in each scallop.

Use a pleating board to make tiny pleats fast.

Center-Stitched
Box Pleats

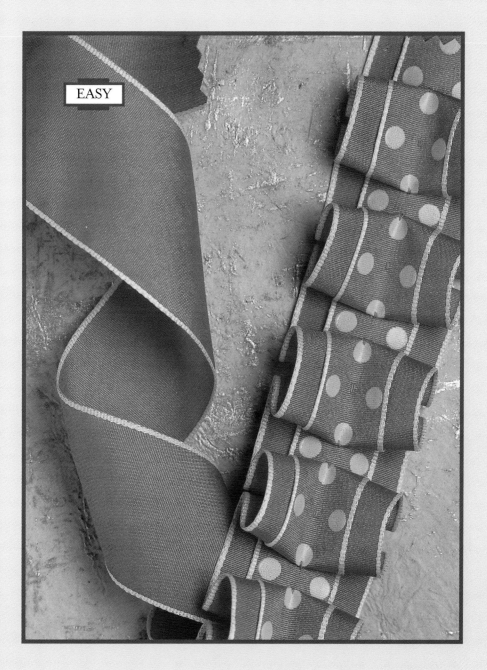

EASY

INSTRUCTIONS

Use a ribbon that's 3X the length of the finished trim. This trim can be machine-stitched.

Center-stitched box pleats can be formed by using either the folded ribbon method or a ruler to measure distances (see "Measuring Ribbon" on p. 10). These pleats cannot be stitched with a gauge in place. The pleats can be stitched with tacks or a continuous running stitch. Tack the pleats as follows.

Tacks

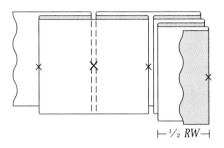

$\vdash \frac{1}{2}\ RW \dashv$

1 Make a stack of two pleats ½ RW wide, as shown.

2 On the wrong side, tack through all layers (there will be three folds on the wrong side).

3 On the front of the ribbon, spread one pleat to the left and one to the right.

4 Tack the outer edges of each pleat in the center of the ribbon.

5 Repeat until the desired length is achieved. To make pleats that touch, place the first fold of the next motif ½ RW from the last fold.

Stitch the pleats with a continuous running stitch as follows.

Continuous stitching

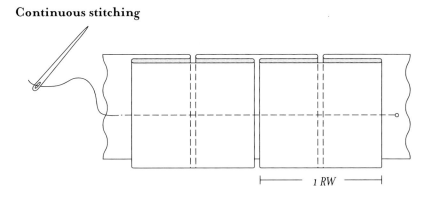

1 Form pleats as directed in "Edge-Stitched Box Pleats" (p. 38), stopping at Step 4.

2 Stitch the pleat in place down the center of the ribbon, using a continuous running stitch.

3 Repeat until the desired length is achieved. To make pleats that touch, place the first fold of the next pleat 1 RW from the last fold.

VARIATIONS

- ◆ Vary the width of the pleats.
- ◆ Vary the distance between pleats.

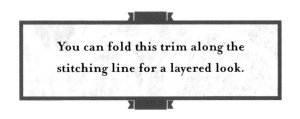

You can fold this trim along the stitching line for a layered look.

Edge-Stitched
Box Pleats

EASY

INSTRUCTIONS

Use a ribbon that's 3X the length of the finished trim. This trim can be machine-stitched.

1 Fold the ribbon right sides together.

2 From the fold, measure ½ RW. Fold the ribbon wrong sides together.

3 From the fold made in Step 2, measure 1 RW. Fold the ribbon wrong sides together again.

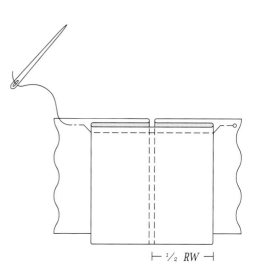

4 Make one last fold, right sides together, positioning it so it just meets the first fold.

5 Stitch the pleat in place along one selvage.

⊢ ½ RW ⊣

6 Repeat until the desired length is achieved. To make pleats that touch, place the first fold of the next pleat 1 RW from the last fold.

VARIATIONS

- ◆ Vary the width of the pleats.
- ◆ Vary the distance between the pleats.

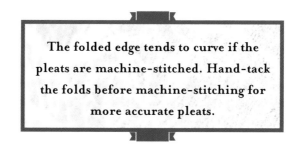

The folded edge tends to curve if the pleats are machine-stitched. Hand-tack the folds before machine-stitching for more accurate pleats.

Box Pleats with Both Edges Stitched

EASY

  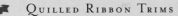

INSTRUCTIONS

Use a ribbon that's 3X the length of the finished trim. This trim can be machine-stitched.

Box pleats with both edges stitched are usually used for insertions, so a continuous stitch can be used because the edgestitching will be covered with fabric or trim. Tacks can be used if they're more appropriate for your application.

Form pleats as directed in "Edge-Stitched Box Pleats" (p. 38). Follow the grain of the ribbon to keep the pleat even from selvage to selvage. In Step 5, stitch the pleats down on the second edge.

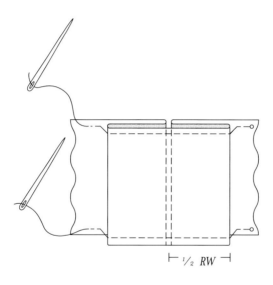

$\vdash \frac{1}{2}\ RW \dashv$

VARIATIONS

- ◆ Leave some space between the pleats.
- ◆ Group pleats, leaving a space between the groups.

Don't press this trim. Pressed pleats flatten out and look like seams.

Edge-Stitched Double and Triple Box Pleats

EASY

INSTRUCTIONS

For double pleats, use a ribbon that's 5X the length of the finished trim. For triple pleats, use a ribbon that's 7X the finished length. This trim can be machine-stitched.

To make a stiff petticoat that will keep the overlying skirt full, stitch overlapping layers of triple box pleats made from a stiff ribbon, such as organdy, to a slip.

Form pleats as directed in "Edge-Stitched Box Pleats" (p. 38), except stack two or three half pleats on one side before proceeding to the adjacent side, as shown. These pleats are normally stitched with a continuous stitch, because the edgestitching is usually covered by fabric or trim. Tacks can be used if they're more appropriate for your application.

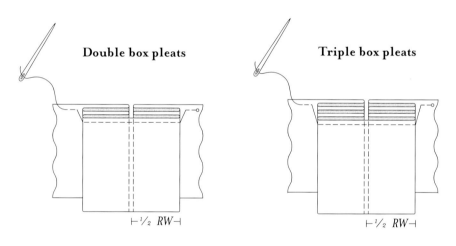

Double box pleats

Triple box pleats

⊢ ½ RW ⊣   ⊢ ½ RW ⊣

VARIATION

◆ Graduate the sizes of the stacked pleats, making the top pleats smaller than the lower ones.

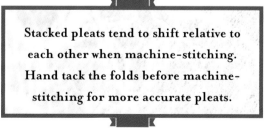

Stacked pleats tend to shift relative to each other when machine-stitching. Hand tack the folds before machine-stitching for more accurate pleats.

Center-Stitched Double and Triple Box Pleats

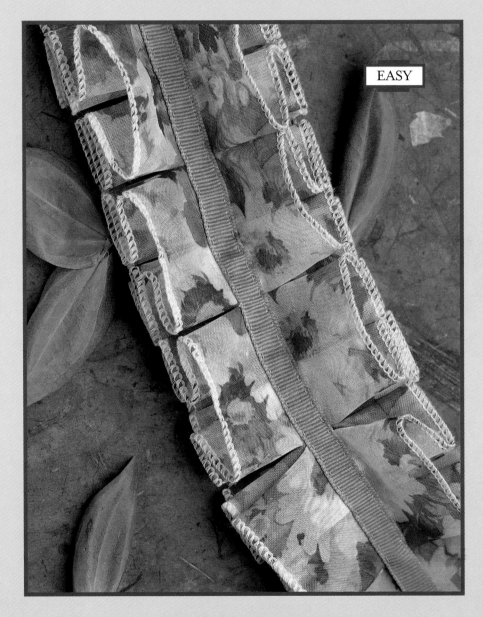

EASY

INSTRUCTIONS

For double pleats, use a ribbon that's 5X the length of the finished trim. For triple pleats, use a ribbon that's 7X the finished length. This trim can be machine-stitched.

Center-stitched double or triple box pleats can be formed by using either the folded ribbon method or a ruler to measure distances (see "Measuring Ribbon" on p. 10). These pleats cannot be stitched with a gauge in place. The pleats can be stitched with tacks or a continuous running stitch. Tack double pleats as follows.

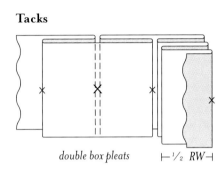

double box pleats ⊢½ RW⊣

1 Make a stack of four pleats ½ RW, as shown.

2 On wrong side, tack through all layers (there will be five folds on wrong side).

3 On front of the ribbon, spread two pleats to the left and two to the right.

4 Tack the outer edges of each stack through all layers in the center of the ribbon.

5 Repeat until the desired length is achieved. To make pleats that touch, place the first fold of the next motif ½ RW from the outer tack.

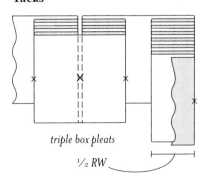

triple box pleats

½ RW

For triple pleats, start with a stack of six pleats. There will be seven folds on the wrong side; on the front of the ribbon, you will spread three folds to each side.

Stitch double and triple pleats with a continuous running stitch as follows.

1 Form pleats as directed in "Edge-Stitched Box Pleats" (p. 38), except stack two or three half pleats on one side before proceeding to the adjacent half.

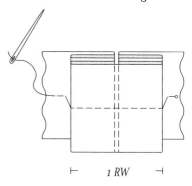

double box pleats

2 Stitch the pleats in place down the center of the ribbon, using a continuous running stitch.

VARIATIONS

Continuous stitching

- ◆ Vary the distance between the pleats.
- ◆ Vary the width of the pleats.
- ◆ Graduate the sizes of the stacked pleats, making the top pleats smaller than the lower ones.

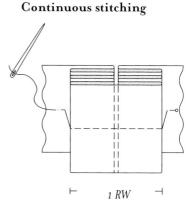

triple box pleats

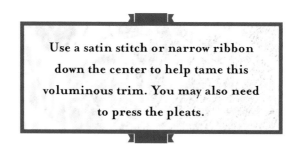

Use a satin stitch or narrow ribbon down the center to help tame this voluminous trim. You may also need to press the pleats.

Paddlewheels

INTERMEDIATE

INSTRUCTIONS

Use a ribbon that's 6X the length of the finished trim. This trim cannot be made using the gauge method of measuring (see "Measuring Ribbon" on p. 10).

1 Make a stack of six pleats ½ RW wide.

2 On the wrong side of the ribbon, tack the pleats together at center and just inside each selvage, as shown (there will be seven folds on the wrong side).

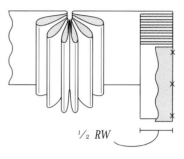

½ RW

3 Flatten the base ribbon, and fan out the pleats on the front of the ribbon.

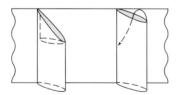

4 Tuck one or both ends of each pleat into the center of the pleat, as shown.

5 Stitch through all folds near the selvage of the base ribbon.

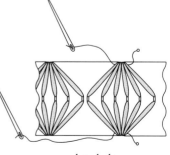

ends tucked in

6 Move along the ribbon 1½ RWs to begin the next paddlewheel. ½ RW will show between motifs.

VARIATIONS

♦ Make the pleats larger or smaller.

♦ Vary the number of pleats in the paddlewheels.

♦ Vary the spacing between the paddlewheels.

♦ Vary the size of the pleats within a single motif. For example, make the outer two pleats large; the middle two, medium; and the center two, small.

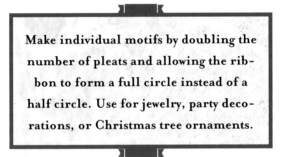

Make individual motifs by doubling the number of pleats and allowing the ribbon to form a full circle instead of a half circle. Use for jewelry, party decorations, or Christmas tree ornaments.

Pulled Box Plaits

INTERMEDIATE

INSTRUCTIONS

For single pleats, use a ribbon that's 3X the length of the finished trim. For double pleats, use a ribbon that's 5X the finished length. For triple pleats, use a ribbon that's 7X the finished length. Center-stitched box pleats can be machine-stitched and then finished by hand.

Make center-stitched single, double, or triple box pleats with either tacks (tacking the outer edges of the pleats is optional) or continuous stitching, as directed in "Center-Stitched Box Pleats" (p. 35) or "Center-Stitched Double and Triple Box Pleats" (p. 44). On the top layer only, pull both selvages together at the center of the pleat until they touch, as shown. Tack together.

Single plaits

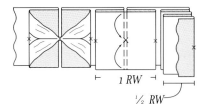

Double plaits

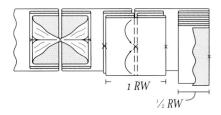

VARIATIONS

- ◆ Space the motifs at various distances along the ribbon.
- ◆ Twist the pleats to 45 degrees; tack only the center of the pleat, or the motif won't twist.
- ◆ Stagger the size of the pleats. For instance, make the top pleat ½ RW wide and the bottom pleat 1 RW.

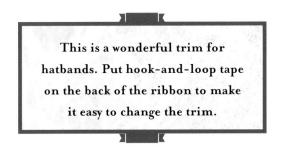

This is a wonderful trim for hatbands. Put hook-and-loop tape on the back of the ribbon to make it easy to change the trim.

Maltese Cross Plaits

INTERMEDIATE

INSTRUCTIONS

Use a ribbon that's 4X the length of the finished trim. The box pleats can be machine-stitched and then finished by hand. This trim cannot be made using the gauge method of measuring (see "Measuring Ribbon" on p. 10).

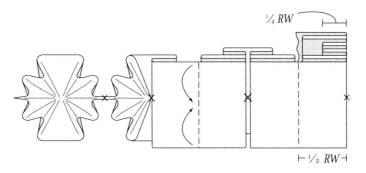

1 Make a stack of four pleats ½ RW, ¼ RW, ¼ RW, and ½ RW wide.

2 Tack the center of the stack on the right side (there will be five folds on the right side).

3 On the back of the ribbon, spread one small and one large pleat to the right and one small and one large pleat to the left.

4 Pull the selvages up between the pleat motifs, and tack them together, as shown.

5 Move ½ RW along ribbon from the last tack to make the first fold of next motif.

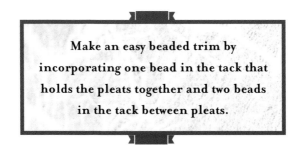

Make an easy beaded trim by incorporating one bead in the tack that holds the pleats together and two beads in the tack between pleats.

Bow Ties

INSTRUCTIONS

Use a ribbon that's 3X the length of the finished trim. This trim cannot be made using the gauge method of measuring (see "Measuring Ribbon" on p. 10). Use buttons, beads, nail heads, ribbon roses, or other small objects to cover the tack in the center of each bow.

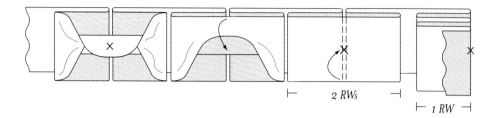

1 Make a stack of two pleats 1 RW wide.

2 On the wrong side, tack the stack in the center, as shown (there will be three folds on the back).

3 On the right side, spread one pleat to the left and one to the right.

4 Fold the top layer of the ribbon into thirds from selvage to selvage, and tack down both sides of the fold on top of first tack.

5 Move along the ribbon 1 RW from the edge of the completed bow tie to begin the next motif.

6 Sew buttons or other small objects over the center tacks.

VARIATIONS

This makes a good trim for men and boys when made in appropriate colors.

- ◆ Twist the bow ties to 45 degrees.
- ◆ Space the bows farther apart.

Tiny Bows

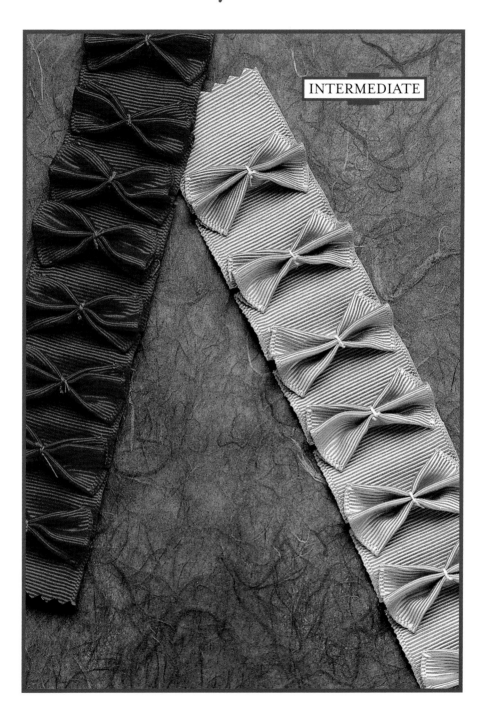

INTERMEDIATE

INSTRUCTIONS

Use a ribbon that's 3X the length of the finished trim. This trim cannot be made using the gauge method of measuring (see "Measuring Ribbon" on p. 10).

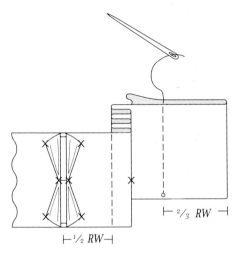

1 Fold the ribbon in half wrong sides together, and stitch across the width of the ribbon $^2/_3$ RW away from the fold (for a $1^1/_2$-in. ribbon, stitch 1 in. from the fold).

2 Fold the loop just made into three even pleats.

3 Tack the pleats together at the center on the right side of the ribbon.

4 Spread the pleats at the selvage edges, and tack the corners of the outer pleats to the ribbon base. The corners will not reach all the way to the selvage of the base ribbon; they will curve in a bit.

5 Leave $^1/_2$ RW between bows.

VARIATION

◆ Space the bows farther apart.

For a fuller trim, add more (four or five) pleats to the bow.

Flying Geese

INTERMEDIATE

INSTRUCTIONS

Use a ribbon that's 3X the length of the finished trim. Measurements must be accurate for the triangles to lie flat. The pleats can be machine-stitched.

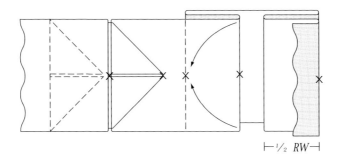

⊢½ *RW*⊣

1 Make a pleat ½ RW wide as directed in "Center-Stitched Knife Pleats" (p. 26).

2 The edge with the fold on top will be the point of the triangle you are forming. Fold the two outer corners of the pleat to the center, forming a triangle; and tack down.

3 Repeat the motif so the triangles just touch.

VARIATION

◆ Vary the spacing between motifs.

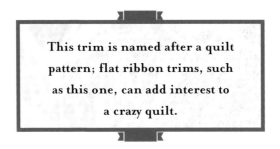

This trim is named after a quilt pattern; flat ribbon trims, such as this one, can add interest to a crazy quilt.

Diamonds and Squares

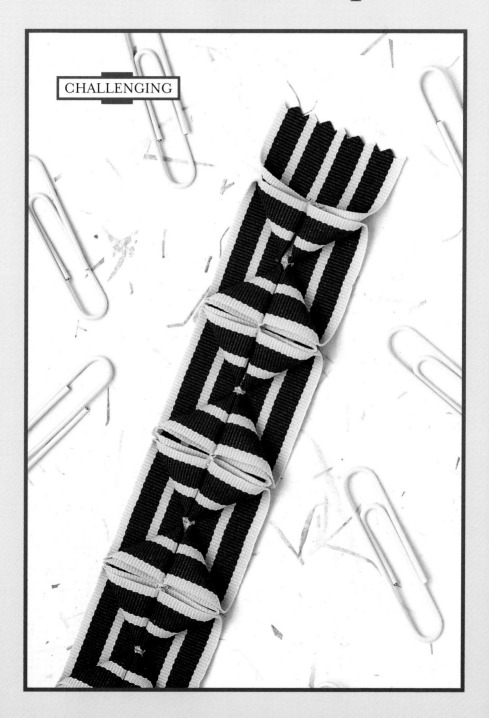

INSTRUCTIONS

Use a ribbon that's 3X the length of the finished trim. Measurement of the pleats must be accurate for the diamonds to fit together properly. The pleats can be machine-stitched.

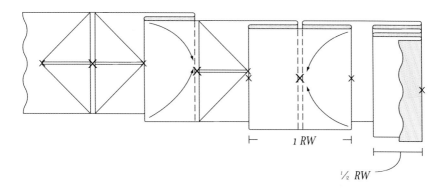

1 Make a box pleat that's just less than 1 RW wide, as directed in "Center-Stitched Box Pleats" (p. 35).

2 Fold the two outer corners of the left pleat to the center and tack.

3 Repeat for the right pleat.

VARIATION

◆ Longitudinally striped ribbon, such as 1½-in. Offray 8271 toffee grosgrain, gives a geometric effect with an optical illusion.

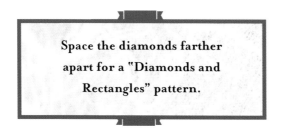

Space the diamonds farther apart for a "Diamonds and Rectangles" pattern.

Hexagons

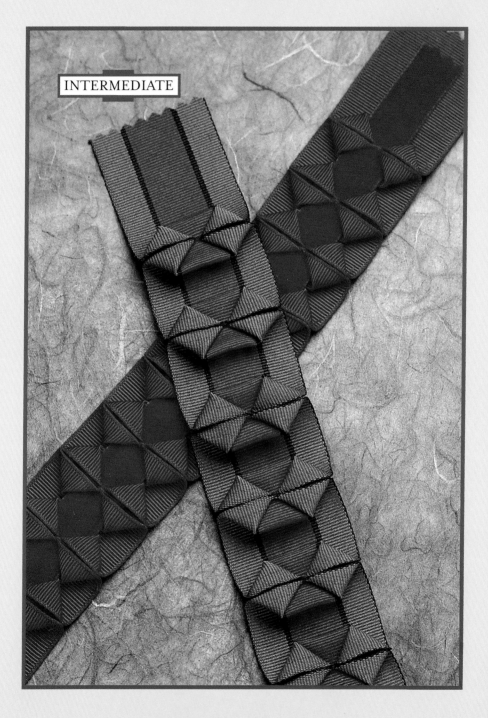

QUILLED RIBBON TRIMS

INSTRUCTIONS

Use a ribbon that's 3X the length of the finished trim.

1 Make a pleat ½ RW wide, as directed in "Center-Stitched Box Pleats" (p. 35). Or fold the ribbon, and stitch from selvage to selvage ½ RW from the fold. (Stitching produces a less flexible trim than does tacking.)

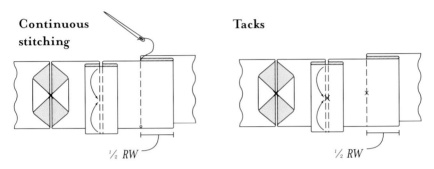

Continuous stitching

Tacks

½ RW   ½ RW

2 Bring both selvages of the box pleat to the center of the ribbon, forming hexagons.

3 Tack the points down in the center.

4 Make the next box pleat 1½ RWs from the first motif, so the finished hexagons are ½ RW apart.

VARIATIONS

- ◆ Offray Status Stripe, which has a wide stripe of contrasting color down the center, is a good choice for this trim.
- ◆ After the box pleats have been made but before the hexagons have been formed, lay a second ribbon that's one-third the width of the pleated ribbon on top of the pleated ribbon. Make the hexagons over the narrower ribbon.
- ◆ Vary the spacing between the hexagons.

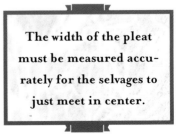

The width of the pleat must be measured accurately for the selvages to just meet in center.

Fans

INTERMEDIATE

INSTRUCTIONS

Use a ribbon that's 2X the length of the finished trim. The folded ribbon method of measuring works well with this trim (see "Measuring Ribbon" on p. 10).

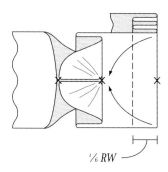

⅙ RW

1 Make a stack of two pleats ⅙ RW wide.

2 On the front, tack the stack in the center (there will be three folds on the front).

3 Pull the selvages together at the fold of the top pleat; tack the selvages together, as shown.

4 Tack that same point to the base ribbon.

5 Repeat for the desired length. Begin the next motif at the last tack.

VARIATIONS

- ◆ Stitch a bead or other small item at the tack that forms the fan.
- ◆ Increasing the size of the pleats (larger than ⅙ RW) gives more fullness to the fan until, at ½ RW, there is enough fullness to form "Arrows" (p. 68).
- ◆ Back to back, these fans form "Rosettes" (p. 66).

This trim produces an interesting radiating effect when made from striped ribbon.

Rosettes

INTERMEDIATE

INSTRUCTIONS

Use a ribbon that's 2½X the length of the finished trim. This trim cannot be made using the gauge method of measuring (see "Measuring Ribbon" on p. 10).

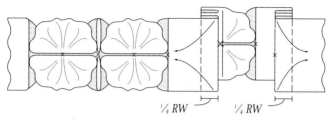

¼ RW   ¼ RW

1 Make a stack of three pleats ¼ RW wide.

2 On the front of the ribbon, tack the stack in the center (there will be four folds on the front).

3 Spread one pleat to the left. Pull the selvages together at the fold of this pleat; tack the selvages together, as shown. Tack the same point to the base ribbon.

4 Tack that same point to the base ribbon.

5 Spread the remaining two pleats to the right. Pull the selvages together at the fold of the top pleat only; tack the selvages together.

6 Tack that same point to the base ribbon in the opposite direction from first pleat, forming a circle. The remaining pleat lies to the back of the trim and is not tacked.

7 Move along the ribbon ½ RW to begin the next rosette.

VARIATION

◆ Stitch a bead or other small object in the center of the motif.

Rosettes really stand out when made with metallic-edged ribbon.

Arrows

INSTRUCTIONS

Use a ribbon that's 3X the length of the finished trim. This trim cannot be made using the gauge method of measuring (see "Measuring Ribbon" on p. 10).

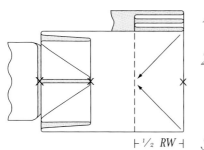

1 Make two pleats ½ RW wide.

2 On the front of the ribbon, tack the stack in the center (there will be three folds on the front).

⊦ ½ RW ⊣

3 Pull the selvages together at the fold of the top pleat; tack the selvages together.

4 Repeat for the desired length of trim. Begin the next motif close to the end of the arrow just finished, leaving enough room to allow the next arrow to lie flat.

VARIATIONS

- ◆ Make three pleats in Step 1, leaving two pleats behind the arrow.
- ◆ Make an additional pleat offset from the first two pleats by ⅛ RW. Pull the selvages of the offset pleat together, and tack. Pull the selvages of the second pleat together, and tack. This forms a double arrow.

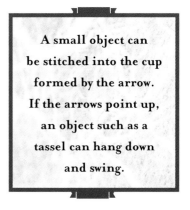

A small object can be stitched into the cup formed by the arrow. If the arrows point up, an object such as a tassel can hang down and swing.

Ruched Ribbon Trims

Ruched ribbon trims are soft and feminine. They are formed by gathering ribbon into decorative patterns. These trims are most effective when either tiny or massive.

The stitching on these trims consists mostly of running stitches. All of the trims can be stitched by hand, and most can be stitched by machine. If you are using wired ribbon and the trim has stitching along the selvage, you can sometimes gather the ribbon on the wire instead of removing the wire and then stitching a gathering line with thread. Wire is too stiff for most garments and needs to be removed if the trim will be used on clothing.

Ruched ribbon trims require a fluid ribbon; stiff ribbons just won't gather up into appealing trims.

Edge Gather

EASY

INSTRUCTIONS

Use a ribbon that's 1½X to 3X the length of the finished trim. This trim can be machine-stitched.

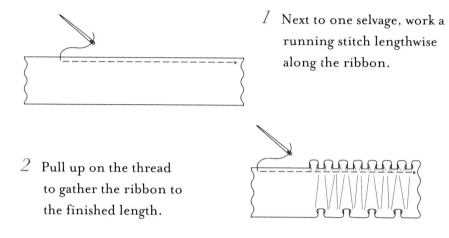

1 Next to one selvage, work a running stitch lengthwise along the ribbon.

2 Pull up on the thread to gather the ribbon to the finished length.

3 Tie off the thread. Adjust the gathers evenly along the length of the ribbon.

VARIATIONS

♦ Layer different widths of ribbon or ribbon and lace and gather as one.

♦ For wired ribbon, remove the wire from one side of the ribbon. Gather the ribbon along the other wire.

♦ Gather near the edge but not right along the selvage.

**Short stitches make a fine ruffle;
long stitches make a full ruffle.**

Center Gather

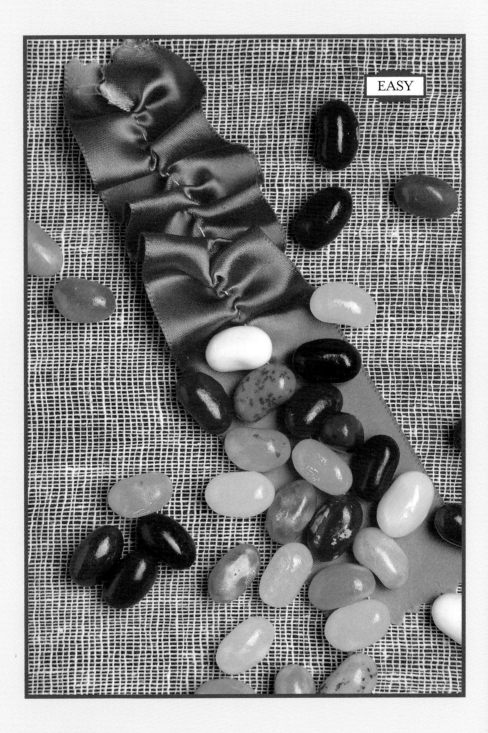

EASY

INSTRUCTIONS

Use a ribbon that's 1½X to 3X the length of the finished trim. This trim can be machine-stitched.

1 Fold the ribbon in half lengthwise and finger-press to mark the stitching line.

2 Work a running stitch lengthwise along the ribbon.

3 Pull up on the thread to gather the ribbon to the finished length.

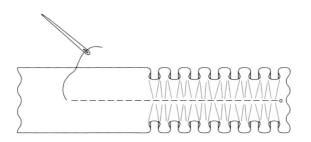

4 Tie off the thread. Adjust the gathers evenly along the length of the ribbon.

VARIATIONS

- ◆ Gather off-center.
- ◆ Fold on the gathered line for a layered look.

Machine-stitch with elastic thread for instant gathers.

Three-Layer Ruffle

EASY

INSTRUCTIONS

Choose three ribbons in graduated widths. Use ribbons that are 1½X to 3X the length of the finished trim. This trim can be machine-stitched. Gathering the three ribbons individually before stitching them together gives a much fuller trim than layering the ribbons first and gathering them as one.

1   Gather each of three ribbons as directed in "Center Gather" (p. 74).

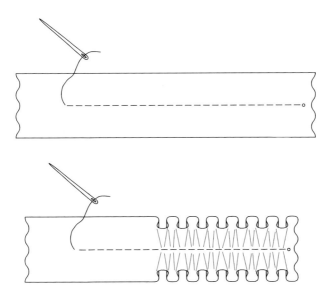

2   Layer the three gathered ribbons, placing the smallest one on top.

3   Line up the gathering threads, and stitch all three ribbons together along the gathering stitches.

VARIATIONS

◆ Vary the number of layers.
◆ Substitute lace for one or more layers.

Use a machine ruffler for a really fast trim.

Multiple Gathers

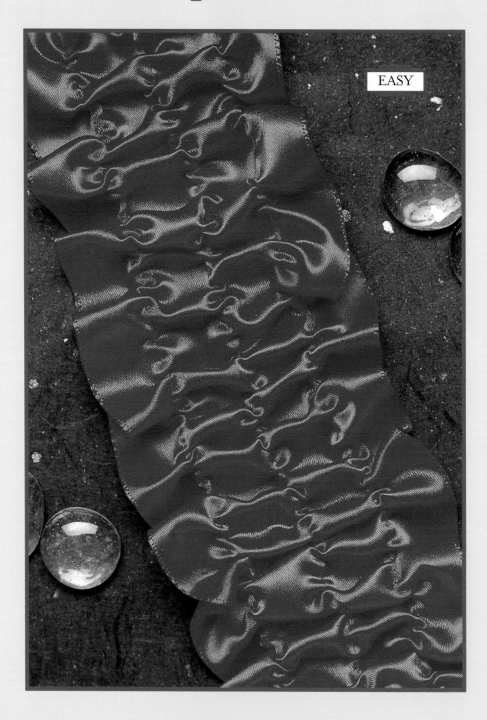

EASY

INSTRUCTIONS

Use a ribbon that's 1½X to 3X the length of the finished trim. This trim can be machine-stitched.

1 Fold the ribbon into thirds lengthwise, and finger-press to mark the stitching lines.

2 Work a running stitch along each stitching line, leaving a 4-in. to 6-in. thread tail.

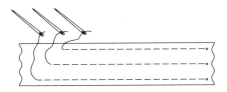

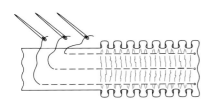

3 Pull up on both thread tails at the same time to gather the ribbon to the finished length.

4 Tie off the threads. Adjust the gathers evenly along the length of the ribbon.

VARIATIONS

- ◆ The gathering lines can be placed any distance apart, depending on the look you want.
- ◆ Stitch a braid down the center of the ribbon over the gathers.
- ◆ Place the gathering lines off-center.
- ◆ Use multiple rows of gathering stitches (see "Shirred Gather" on p. 82).

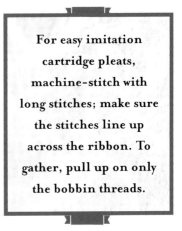

For easy imitation cartridge pleats, machine-stitch with long stitches; make sure the stitches line up across the ribbon. To gather, pull up on only the bobbin threads.

Gathers and Spaces

INSTRUCTIONS

Use a ribbon that's 4X the length of the finished trim.

1 Fold the ribbon in half lengthwise, and finger-press to mark the stitching line.

2 Work a running stitch along the stitching line for 3 RWs.

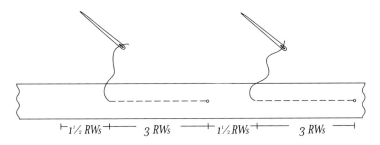

3 Pull up on the thread to gather the ribbon. Tie off the thread.

4 Move 1½ RWs along the ribbon and repeat Steps 1 to 3.

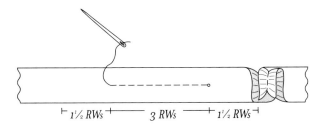

5 Twist the gathers neatly into an S shape.

VARIATION

♦ Vary the spacing between motifs.

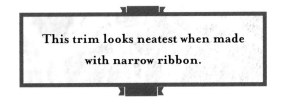

This trim looks neatest when made with narrow ribbon.

Shirred Gather

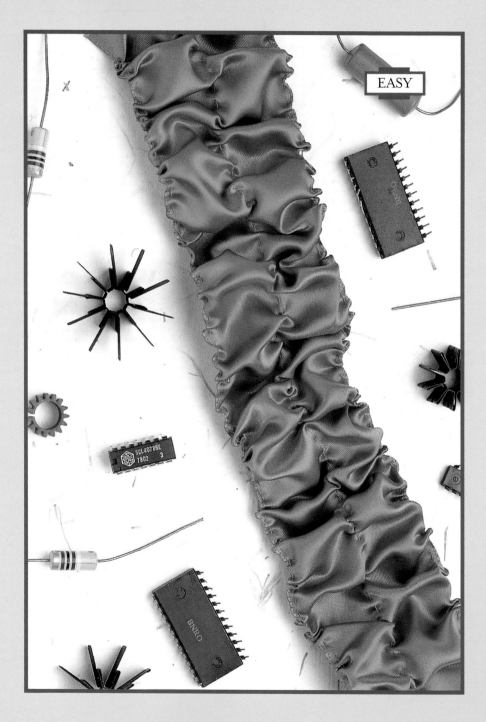

EASY

INSTRUCTIONS

Use a ribbon that's 2X to 3X the length of the finished trim. This trim can be machine-stitched.

1 Fold the ribbon in half lengthwise, and finger-press to mark the center stitching line.

2 Work a running stitch along the center stitching line and one just inside each selvage, leaving a 4-in. to 6-in. thread tail on each stitching line.

3 When all three lines have been stitched, pull up on all thread tails at once, gathering the ribbon to the desired fullness.

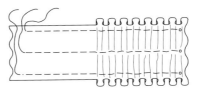

4 Tie off the threads. Adjust the gathers evenly along the ribbon.

VARIATIONS

- ◆ Use more lines of gathering on wider ribbons.
- ◆ For a puffier trim, mark parallel lines on the item being trimmed that are closer together than the stitching lines on the trim. Attach the ribbon trim by matching the stitching lines to the marked lines.

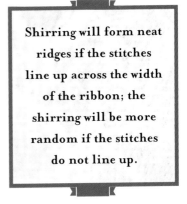

Shirring will form neat ridges if the stitches line up across the width of the ribbon; the shirring will be more random if the stitches do not line up.

Shells

EASY

INSTRUCTIONS

Use a ribbon that's 2X the length of the finished trim. This trim can be machine-stitched.

1 Fold the ribbon at 45 degrees. Finger-press.

2 Starting at one edge, make short running stitches along the fold line.

3 When you reach the other edge of the ribbon, fold the ribbon at 45 degrees, starting where the stitching meets the edge. Continue stitching along the new fold line.

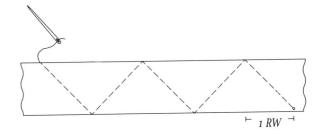

$\vdash$ *1 RW* $\dashv$

4 Repeat, creating a zigzag stitching line down the ribbon.

5 Pull up on the thread to gather the ribbon.

6 Tie off the thread. Adjust the gathers evenly along the ribbon. Cup the shells up or down as desired.

VARIATION
   ◆ Fill the center of the shells with ribbon flowers or beads.

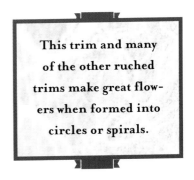

This trim and many of the other ruched trims make great flowers when formed into circles or spirals.

Half-Shells

EASY

RUCHED RIBBON TRIMS

INSTRUCTIONS

Use a ribbon that's 2X the length of the finished trim. This trim can be machine-stitched.

The pattern of the stitching lines for this trim results in a one-sided shell. Form the trim as directed in "Shells" (p. 84), except use the stitching pattern shown here.

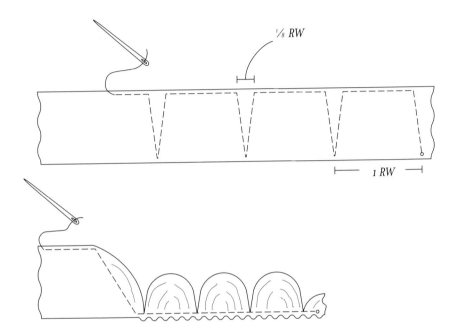

VARIATION

◆ Change the shape of the stitching line to create shells with different shapes.

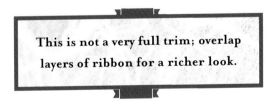

This is not a very full trim; overlap layers of ribbon for a richer look.

Scalloped Edge

RUCHED RIBBON TRIMS

INSTRUCTIONS

Use a ribbon that's 1½X the length of the finished trim. This trim can be machine-stitched.

1 Along both edges of the ribbon, mark a zigzag pattern that is ¼ RW high by ½ RW wide, as shown. Match the points of the zigzags at opposite selvages.

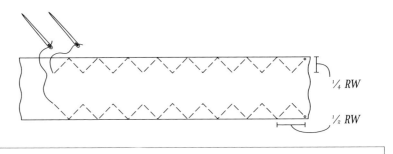

2 Use a short running stitch to stitch along the zigzags, leaving a 4-in. to 6-in. thread tail on each side.

3 Pull up on the thread tails to form scallops. This will gather the center of the ribbon at the same time.

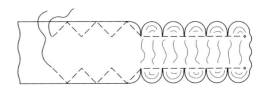

4 Tie off the threads. Adjust the scallops.

VARIATIONS

- Make the zigzags taller.
- Add one or more rows of gathering (shirring) down the center of the ribbon.

> **Because the stitching pattern includes many turns, it is faster to stitch this trim by hand than by machine.**

Semicircles

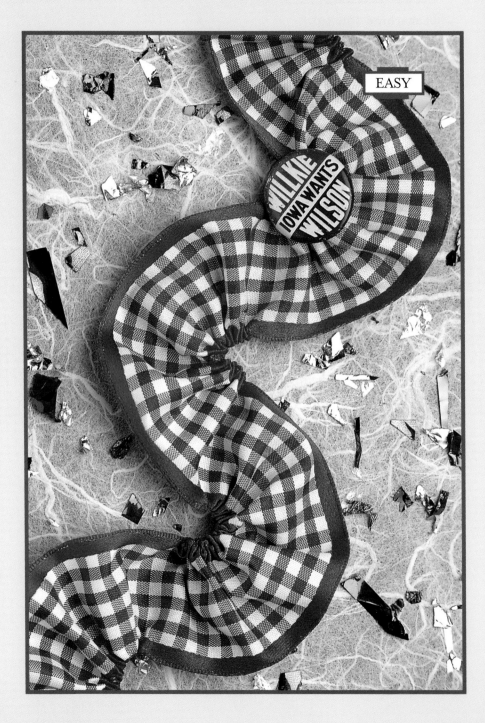

EASY

RUCHED RIBBON TRIMS

INSTRUCTIONS

Use a ribbon that's 3X the length of the finished trim. This trim can be machine-stitched.

1   Knot the thread along the selvage of the ribbon.

2   Make short running stitches along selvage for 3 RWs.

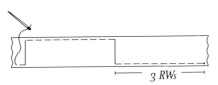

3 RWs

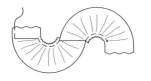

3   Pull up on the thread until the gathers are packed as tightly as possible. Tie off the thread with a knot on wrong side of the ribbon. Do not cut the thread.

4   Cross the width of the ribbon on the back, and knot the thread at the opposite selvage.

5   Make short running stitches for 3 RWs, pull on the thread to gather the stitches tightly, and tie off the thread.

6   Cross the back of the ribbon, and repeat for the desired length.

VARIATIONS

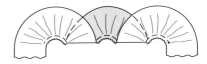

- ◆ Use more than 3 RWs for a ruffled semicircle.
- ◆ Fold every other semicircle along the threads that cross the ribbon so that all the semicircles are on one side.

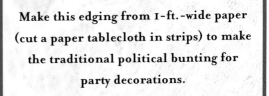

Make this edging from 1-ft.-wide paper (cut a paper tablecloth in strips) to make the traditional political bunting for party decorations.

Tucked Gather

RUCHED RIBBON TRIMS

INSTRUCTIONS

Use a ribbon that's 1½X to 3X the length of the finished trim. This trim can be machine-stitched.

1 Fold the ribbon in half lengthwise wrong sides together.

2 Place short running stitches ⅛ in. (or as desired) from the fold line.

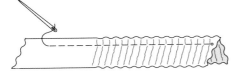

End view

3 Press the ribbon into a W shape, using the stitching line as fold lines.

stitching

Fold to press.

4 Pull up on the thread to gather the ribbon.

5 Tie off the thread. Adjust the gathers evenly along the ribbon.

VARIATIONS

- ◆ Make the tuck wider.
- ◆ Make multiple rows of tucks.
- ◆ Don't gather the tucks.
- ◆ Make tucks without gathers across the width or diagonally across the ribbon.

Use a machine-stitched shell hem for a "Scalloped Tucked Gather."

Corded Gather

INSTRUCTIONS

Use a ribbon that's 1½X to 3X the length of the finished trim. Cut a piece of piping cord to the length of the ribbon. Try ⁵⁄₃₂-in. cord for 1½-in. ribbon. This trim can be machine-stitched, using a zipper foot.

1 Fold the ribbon in half lengthwise, wrong sides together, around the cord.

2 Tack the cord to the ribbon at one end.

3 Make short run-
ning stitches
through the rib-
bon next to the

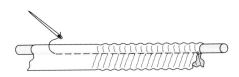

cord, as shown. Be careful not to catch the cord in the stitches.

4 Press the flat edges of the ribbon open.

5 Pull up on the thread to
gather the ribbon along
the cord.

6 Tie off the thread. Tack the remaining end of the cord to the rib-bon. Adjust the gathers evenly along the cord.

VARIATION

♦ Use smaller or larger cord relative to the size of the ribbon.

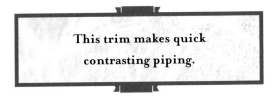

**This trim makes quick
contrasting piping.**

Beading

RUCHED RIBBON TRIMS

INSTRUCTIONS

Use a ribbon that's 1¼X the length of the finished trim. This trim can be machine-stitched.

1 With small running stitches, stitch across the width of the ribbon.

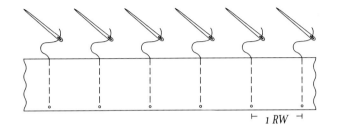

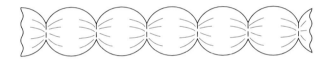

2 Pull up on the thread until the gathers are packed as tightly as possible. Tie off the thread.

3 Move 1 RW along the ribbon and repeat.

VARIATIONS

- ◆ Make the gathers 1½ or 2 RWs apart for oval beads.
- ◆ Push the beads close together so they overlap and lie in one direction.
- ◆ Wrap braid or cord around the gathers.

Stuff the beads with batting, cotton balls, wooden beads to prevent crushing. Select stuffing that is compatible with the use of the trim.

- ◆ Mark a straight line on the item being trimmed, and center beads over the line. Attach the trim in a zigzag, so the gathers alternate above and below the marked line.

Circles and Dots

EASY

RUCHED RIBBON TRIMS

INSTRUCTIONS

Use a ribbon that's 1½X the length of the finished trim. A gauge is used to draw the circles, but any method of measuring can be used to mark the centers of the circles (see "Measuring Ribbon" on p. 10).

1 Make a paper circle pattern that is ¼ in. less in diameter than the RW.

2 Mark the center of a circle every 2 RWs along the ribbon.

3 Place the circle pattern over the first mark, centering the pattern so that is ⅛ in. from each selvage; trace the outline.

4 Stitch around the circle with small running stitches.

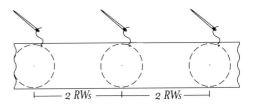

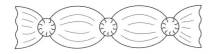

5 Pull up on the thread to gather the circle into a dot (or puff).

6 Stuff the dot with batting, if desired. Tie off the thread.

7 Move to next mark, and repeat.

VARIATIONS

♦ Make the dots farther apart. The space between the dots will be oval, not circular.

♦ Stitch a bead or other small object to the center of each dot.

Use as a decorative header for tassels or fringe.

Flutes

INTERMEDIATE

INSTRUCTIONS

Use a ribbon that's 3X the length of the finished trim. The flutes look best when the ribbon is at least 2¼ in. wide.

1 Measure and mark ¼ RW from the selvage along each edge of the ribbon.

2 Beginning at one end, make a ¼ RW pleat across the width of the ribbon, and stitch between the marked lines. Tie off the thread.

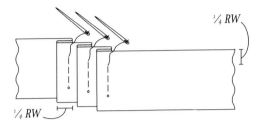

3 Finger-press the pleat into a cylinder or flute.

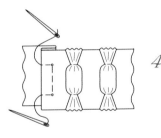

4 Stitch across the top of the flute (just the cylinder part) along the marked line.

5 Pull up on the thread to gather the top of the flute. Tie off the thread.

6 Repeat at other end of the flute. Move ⅓ RW along the ribbon, and begin the next flute.

VARIATION

◆ Make the flutes closer together or farther apart.

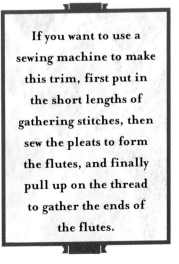

If you want to use a sewing machine to make this trim, first put in the short lengths of gathering stitches, then sew the pleats to form the flutes, and finally pull up on the thread to gather the ends of the flutes.

Ribbons and Bows

INTERMEDIATE

 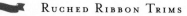

INSTRUCTIONS

Use a ribbon that's 2X the length of the finished trim. Cut a length of soutache or other small braid to 1¼X the finished length. Use a heavy thread or double thread when gathering these multiple layers. This trim can be machine-stitched.

1 Start with a large bow. Fold the ribbon into a 3-RW-wide box pleat, placing the folds at the center back and overlapping the folds by ¼ in., as shown.

2 Using a running stitch, stitch across the center of the box pleat from selvage to selvage. Make sure you catch both folds on the back (you will stitch through five layers of ribbon).

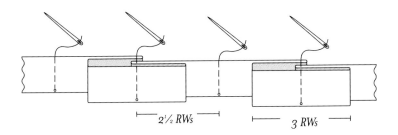

3 Pull up on the thread to gather the ribbon. Tie off the thread.

4 Next make a small bow. Move 2½ RWs along the ribbon from the stitching line. Using a running stitch, stitch across the ribbon through one layer.

5 Pull up on the thread to gather the ribbon. Tie off the thread.

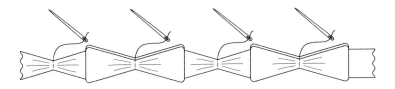

6 Move 2½ RWs along ribbon from the last stitching line. This is the center back of the next large bow.

7 Repeat for the desired number of bows.

8 Lay the soutache braid behind the gathers of the first bow. Wrap the braid around the gathers three times.

9 Stitch the braid in place on the back of the ribbon.

10 Move to the next bow and repeat. Do not cut the braid between the bows, because most braids ravel badly.

VARIATION
♦ Vary the distance between the bows.

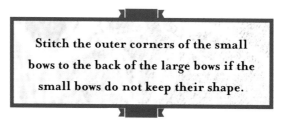

Stitch the outer corners of the small bows to the back of the large bows if the small bows do not keep their shape.

Smocked and Looped Ribbon Trims

Although only two examples each of the smocked and looped trims are shown, the techniques produce wonderful trims. Smocked trims are loosely based on gathering techniques. Looped trims are more closely related to twisted trims.

Smocking is a group of stitches that are pulled together and knotted. For these trims, the smocking stitches are hidden on the reverse of the ribbon, so only the pulled design of the ribbon itself shows. Ribbons for smocking must be soft and supple; satins and taffetas are ideal.

Looped ribbon trims are created by looping the ribbon back through itself. Stiff ribbons that hold their shape are best for these trims; narrow ribbons work better than wide ones. No stitching is used on these trims.

Shell Smocking

EASY

INSTRUCTIONS

Use a ribbon that's 1½X the length of the finished trim.

1   On the back, take a stitch through the ribbon at one selvage.

2   Move down the ribbon ½ RW, and take a stitch in the center of the ribbon.

3   Take a third stitch parallel to the first stitch at the opposite selvage, as shown.

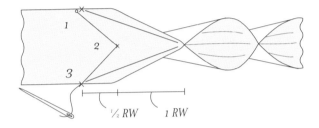

4   Pull up on the thread so all three stitches come together, and knot in place.

5   Lay the thread along the selvage of the ribbon 1 RW from the first stitch.

6   Take a stitch, and knot the thread in place. Do not pull the thread tight before knotting.

7   Repeat Steps 1 to 6, until the desired length is achieved.

VARIATION

♦ Make the shells closer together or farther apart.

> **Victorians used this trim on silk blouses.**

Lattice Smocking

INSTRUCTIONS

Use a ribbon that's 1¼X
the length of the finished trim.
Use a wide ribbon for best effect.

1 On the back of the ribbon, mark
a grid of dots ¼ in. by ¼ in.

Lattice pattern

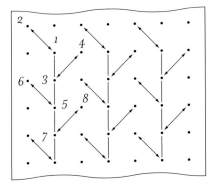

Pulled stitch for smocking

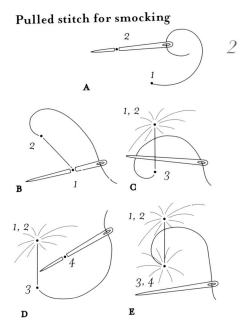

2 On the back of the ribbon, stitch
the smocking pattern across width
of ribbon, following the diagrams. Using small stitches, take a
stitch through the ribbon at 1 and
then at 2. Take another stitch at 1.
Pull 1 and 2 together so they
touch. Take a stitch at 3 and form
a slip knot around the thread, as
shown. Take a stitch at 4 and
another stitch at 3. Pull 3 and 4
together. Continue alternating
between slip-knotted stitches and
pulled stitches.

VARIATION

◆ There are several lattice smocking patterns available. Refer to an
embroidery book that discusses lattice smocking or North
American smocking.

This trim makes a wonderful shawl collar.

Looped Ribbon

INTERMEDIATE

SMOCKED AND LOOPED RIBBON TRIMS

INSTRUCTIONS

Use a ribbon that's 6X the length of the finished trim.

1 Form a loop in the end of the ribbon 1 RW wide, and secure it with a knot or stitch.

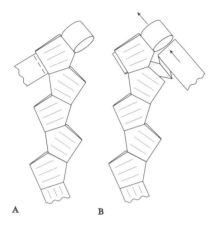

A   B

2 Fold the ribbon to the back, form a new loop by folding the ribbon in half, and push the new loop through the previous loop.

3 Adjust the size of the new loop to 1 RW wide.

4 Repeat, folding and pushing in the opposite direction for the next loop.

VARIATION

♦ Hold two different colored ribbons together and treat them as one to create a two-colored trim.

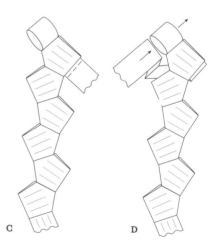

C   D

This is a dressy version of rick rack.

Two-Ribbon Looped Trim

INTERMEDIATE

INSTRUCTIONS

Use ribbons that are 4X the length of the finished trim. This trim requires two ribbons.

1 Make a loop 1 RW wide in the end of one ribbon, and stitch or knot it in place.

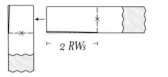

2 Make a loop 2 RW wide in the second ribbon, and stitch or knot it in place.

3 Slip the 2-RW loop through the 1-RW loop.

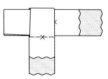

4 Fold the 1-RW ribbon back.

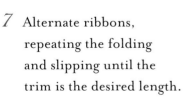

Fold back.

5 Fold the ribbon in half, and slip the fold through the loop at the top of the trim, forming a new loop.

6 Tighten the previous loop to 1 RW, if necessary.

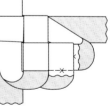

7 Alternate ribbons, repeating the folding and slipping until the trim is the desired length.

VARIATION

◆ Use two ribbons of different widths.

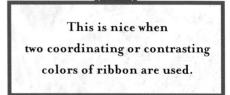

This is nice when two coordinating or contrasting colors of ribbon are used.

Twisted Ribbon Trims

Twisted ribbon trims are formed by twisting and folding ribbon continually in one direction (usually) and tacking the twists in place. These trims have a bold, geometric look.

Firmly woven or stiff ribbons are required for making twisted ribbon trims. Soft ribbons won't hold the twisted shape. My favorite ribbons for these trims are grosgrain and taffeta with metallic threads.

Twisted ribbon trims can be formed in hand or with the aid of gauges. Trims formed in hand without pressing have a softer look. When formed with gauges, the folds are pressed into the ribbon, creating a crisp, tailored look.

The reverse sides of these twisted trims are as decorative as the fronts.

Making Twisted Ribbon Trims

FOR TRIMS MADE IN HAND, the ribbon is twisted and adjusted until the shape is pleasing. Matching up twists and folds to RW measurements helps keep the twists consistent as the trim is formed. The trim can be pressed for a crisp look after the twists are tacked in place.

Gauges cut into polygon shapes can also be used to make twisted ribbon trims. To make the gauges, twist a short length of ribbon as shown in the directions until the shape pleases you. Steam press until the folds are well creased. Unfold the ribbon and cut the shapes apart along the fold lines. To make the gauges, trace the shapes onto lightweight card stock or a plastic that will not melt. Lay a gauge on the ribbon, fold the ribbon over the gauge, and press the fold in place. Remove the gauge, refold the ribbon along the pressed fold, insert the next gauge, and repeat. After a few folds have been completed, tack the twists in place.

In the diagrams for the twisted trims, a solid line indicates that the fold is made toward you and a dashed line means that the fold is made away from you.

Zigzag Twist

INSTRUCTIONS

Use a ribbon that's 1⅓X the length of the finished trim.

1 Make folds in the ribbon as shown. The ribbon always twists in the same direction.

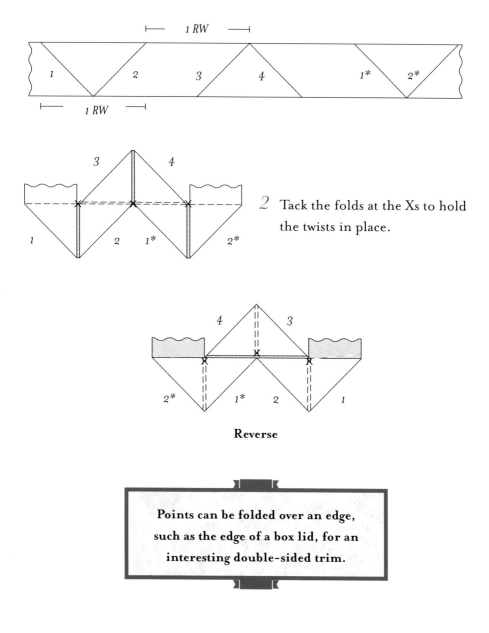

2 Tack the folds at the Xs to hold the twists in place.

Reverse

> **Points can be folded over an edge, such as the edge of a box lid, for an interesting double-sided trim.**

Ribbon Prairie Points

INTERMEDIATE

INSTRUCTIONS

Use a ribbon that's 1⅓X the length of the finished trim.

1 Make folds in the ribbon as shown. The ribbon twists in one direction for folds 1 and 2 and in the opposite direction for folds 3 and 4.

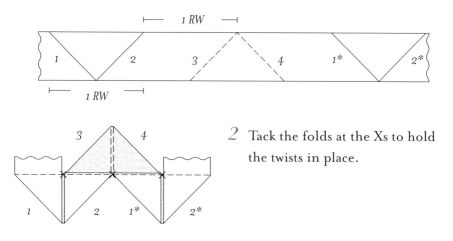

2 Tack the folds at the Xs to hold the twists in place.

3 Finally, fold every other point up along the center line so the tips all point in the same direction. Alternately, you can fold each point up as it is formed.

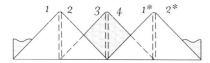
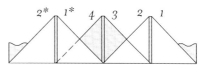

Reverse with alternate folding pattern

Unlike fabric prairie points, there are no cut, raw edges with ribbon prairie points; so this can be laundered repeatedly without the edges raveling or coming untucked.

Diamond Fence Rail

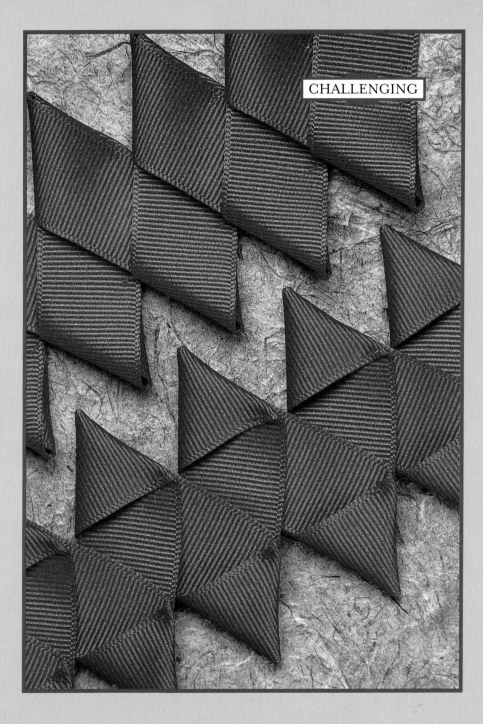

CHALLENGING

Twisted Ribbon Trims

INSTRUCTIONS

Use a ribbon that's 5X the length of the finished trim. This trim can be machine-stitched down the center, but the stitching detracts from the finished look of the trim.

1 Fold the ribbon as shown.

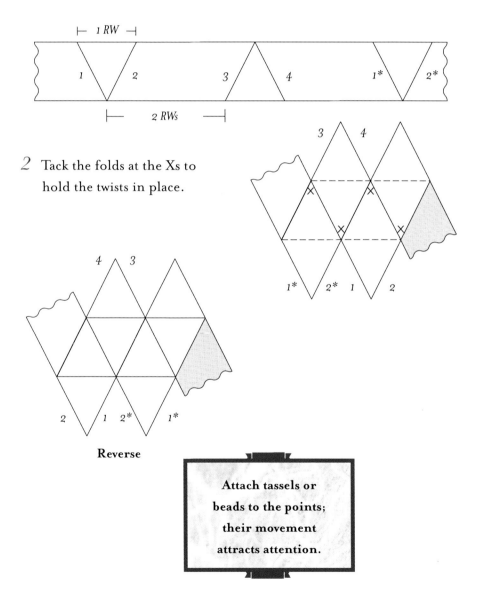

2 Tack the folds at the Xs to hold the twists in place.

Reverse

Attach tassels or
beads to the points;
their movement
attracts attention.

Square Fence Rail

CHALLENGING

INSTRUCTIONS

Use a ribbon that's $3\frac{1}{2}$X the length of the finished trim. This trim can be machine-stitched down the center, but the stitching detracts from the finished look of the trim.

1 Make folds in the ribbon as shown.

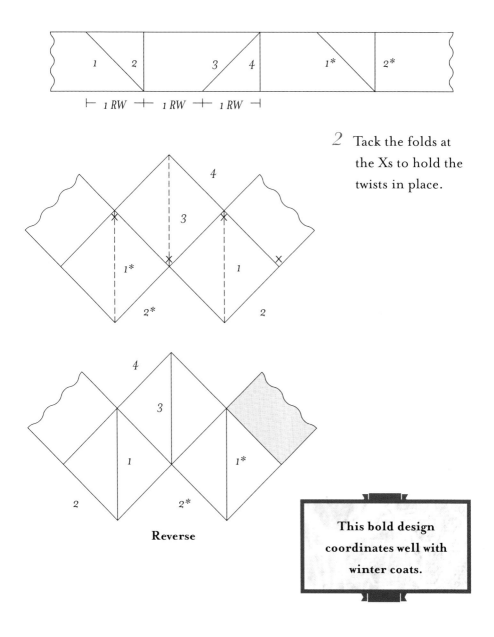

2 Tack the folds at the Xs to hold the twists in place.

Reverse

This bold design coordinates well with winter coats.

Alternating Stripes

INSTRUCTIONS

Use a ribbon that's 3X the length of the finished trim. Striped ribbons show off this twisted pattern especially well.

1 Make folds in the ribbon as shown.

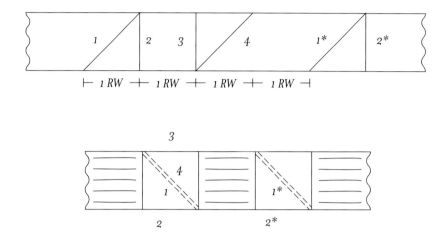

2 On the back, stitch the diagonal folds together. Tack the folds at the four corners, if necessary.

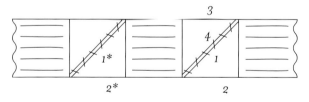

Reverse

This is a good trim for men and boys
when done in appropriate colors.

Shark's Teeth

CHALLENGING

INSTRUCTIONS

Use a ribbon that's 3X the length of the finished trim.

1 Make folds in the ribbon as shown.

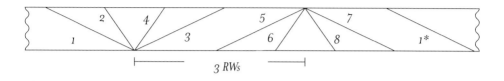

2 Tack the folds at the Xs to hold the twists in place. Intermediate tacks may be necessary on stiff ribbons.

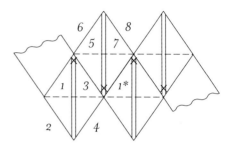

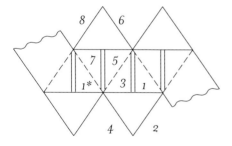

Reverse

3 If you choose to use the reverse side of this trim, you may want to move the tacks slightly so they are less conspicuous.

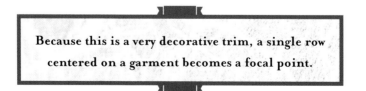

Because this is a very decorative trim, a single row centered on a garment becomes a focal point.

Sources

MOST OF THE RIBBONS USED IN THIS BOOK were purchased at retail outlets of major sewing and craft stores. Like clothing, ribbon colors and styles change season to season, so you may not be able to find the exact ribbons used here. If you would like to shop for ribbon by mail or on the Internet, D and J Hobby carries a huge assortment of current ribbons from several manufacturers:

D and J Hobby and Crafts
96 San Thomas Aquino Rd.
Campbell, CA 95008
(408) 279-1696
www.djhobby.com

For more specialized companies that do retail mail order, try these:

M & J Trimming Co., Inc.
1000 Sixth Ave.
New York, NY 10018
(212) 391-6200
www.mjtrim.com
Basic and novelty ribbons

Ribbon Hood Co.
668 Texas Ave.
York, PA 17404
(888) 854-0914
www.users.aol.com/
ribbonhood/ribbhood.htm
Satins, sheers, metallics,
printed ribbons

Renaissance Ribbons
9690 Stackhouse Rd.
P.O. Box 699
Oregon House, CA 95962
(530) 692-0842
www.rribbons.com
Rayon, cotton, grosgrain,
silk ribbons

Tinsel Trading Co.
47 W. 38th St.
New York, NY 10018
(212) 730-1030
Vintage ribbons

Look for these and other Taunton Press titles at your local bookstore. You can order them direct by calling (800) 888-8286 or by visiting our website at www.taunton.com. Call for a free catalog.

Sewing for Plus Sizes

Embellishments A to Z

Fabric Savvy

Linen and Cotton

Sewing Basics

Scarves to Make

Fine Embellishment Techniques

Just Pockets

Sew the New Fleece

The Sewing Machine Guide

Fine Machine Sewing

50 Heirloom Buttons to Make

Couture Sewing Techniques

Shirtmaking

Beyond the Pattern

Distinctive Details

Fit and Fabric

Fitting Solutions

Fitting Your Figure

Great Quilting Techniques

Great Sewn Clothes

Jackets, Coats and Suits

Quilts and Quilting

Sewing Tips & Trade Secrets

Stitchery and Needle Lace

Techniques for Casual Clothes

Ribbon Knits

The Jean Moss Book of
World Knits

The Knit Hat Book

Knitted Sweater Style

Knitting Tips & Trade Secrets

Hand-Manipulated Stitches
for Machine Knitters

Alice Starmore's Book of
Fair Isle Knitting

Great Knits

Hand-Knitting Techniques

Knitting Around the World

Colorful Knitwear Design

American Country Needlepoint

SEWING COMPANION LIBRARY

Easy Guide to Sewing Tops
& T-Shirts

Easy Guide to Sewing Blouses

Easy Guide to Sewing Jackets

Easy Guide to Sewing Linings

Easy Guide to Sewing Pants

Easy Guide to Sewing Skirts

Easy Guide to Serging Fine
Fabrics